The Bill of Rights

Amendment I

Congress shall make no law respecting an establishment of religion, or prohibiting the free exercise thereof; or abridging the freedom of speech, or of the press; or the right of the people peaceably to assemble, and to petition the Government for a redress of grievances.

Amendment II

A well regulated Militia, being necessary to the security of a free State, the right of the people to keep and bear Arms, shall not be infringed.

Amendment III

No Soldier shall, in time of peace be quartered in any house, without the consent of the Owner, nor in time of war, but in a manner to be prescribed by law.

Amendment IV

The right of the people to be secure in their persons, houses, papers, and effects, against unreasonable searches and seizures, shall not be violated, and no Warrants shall issue, but upon probable cause, supported by Oath or affirmation, and particularly describing the place to be searched, and the persons or things to be seized.

Amendment V

No person shall be held to answer for a capital, or otherwise infamous crime, unless on a presentment or indictment of a Grand Jury, except in cases arising in the land or naval forces, or in the Militia, when in actual service in time of War or public danger; nor shall any person be subject for the same offence to be twice put in jeopardy of life or limb; nor shall be compelled in any criminal case to be a witness against himself, nor be deprived of life, liberty, or property, without due process of law; nor shall private property be taken for public use, without just compensation.

Amendment VI

In all criminal prosecutions, the accused shall enjoy the right to a speedy and public trial, by an impartial jury of the State and district wherein the crime shall have been committed, which district shall have been previously ascertained by law, and to be informed of the nature and cause of the accusation; to be confronted with the witnesses against him; to have compulsory process for obtaining witnesses in his favor, and to have the Assistance of Counsel for his defence.

Amendment VII

In Suits at common law, where the value in controversy shall exceed twenty dollars, the right of trial by jury shall be preserved, and no fact tried by a jury, shall be otherwise re-examined in any Court of the United States, than according to the rules of the common law.

Amendment VIII

Excessive bail shall not be required, nor excessive fines imposed, nor cruel and unusual punishments inflicted.

Amendment IX

The enumeration in the Constitution, of certain rights, shall not be construed to deny or disparage others retained by the people.

Amendment X

The powers not delegated to the United States by the Constitution, nor prohibited by it to the States, are reserved to the States respectively, or to the people.

FIREARMS MANUFACTURING
ACQUISITION AND DEPOSITION RECORDS

RECORD BOOK NO. ______________________

CONTINUED FROM RECORD BOOK NO. __________ START ON DATE __________

CONTINUED TO RECORD BOOK NO. __________ END ON DATE __________

ASSIGNED TO:

NAME ______________________

SIGNATURE ______________________ DATE ______________________

DATE ISSUED ______________________ BY ______________________

PHONE ______________________ EMAIL ______________________

COMPANY ______________________

DEPARTMENT ______________________

ADDRESS ______________________

CITY ______________________

STATE ____________

ZIP ____________

OTHER IMPORTANT INFORMATION

FFL LIC. NO. ______________________

TAX / EIN NO. ______________________

NAICS ______________________

DUNS ______________________

Firearms Manufacturing - Acquisition and Disposition Bound Book
Firearms Transfer Bound Book for 07 FFL Manufacturers, 1000 Record Entry A & D Ledger with Regulations Quick Reference
Hard Cover

The *Bill of Rights* and excerpts from *Title 27 of the Code of Federal Regulations* are courtesy of The National Archive

For publisher information:

Cabin in the Woods Publishers, LLC
info@cabininthewoodspublishers.com
cabininthewoodspublishers.com

For FFL information:

Sanctuary Armaments LLC
sales@sanctuaryarmaments.com
sanctuaryarmaments.com

Note from Editor

When interacting and complying with any federal, state, or local regulatory or law enforcement agency, it is the responsibility of the Federal Firearm Licensee (FFL) to perform its due diligence regarding statues, regulations, laws, rulings, and ordinances. The referenced codes and regulations should not be considered an exhaustive or legally binding text. Instead, should be viewed as a reference when conducting business as a firearms dealer or manufacturer.

The following regulations are excerpts from the Department of Justice Bureau of Alcohol, Tobacco, Firearms, and Explosives Rules and Regulations (effective 1/31/2023). Since definitions and expectations regarding firearms are often subject to change, this reference is provided "as is" with no warranty. For complete and current regulations, visit: https://regulations.atf.gov/

27 CFR Part 478 – Regulations: Selected References

§ 478.11 Meaning of terms

Collector.

Any person who acquires, holds, or disposes of firearms as curios or relics.

Curios or relics.

Firearms which are of special interest to collectors by reason of some quality other than is associated with firearms intended for sporting use or as offensive or defensive weapons. To be recognized as curios or relics, firearms must fall within one of the following categories:

a. Firearms which were manufactured at least 50 years prior to the current date, but not including replicas thereof;

b. Firearms which are certified by the curator of a municipal, State, or Federal museum which exhibits firearms to be curios or relics of museum interest; and

c. Any other firearms which derive a substantial part of their monetary value from the fact that they are novel, rare, bizarre, or because of their association with some historical figure, period, or event. Proof of qualification of a particular firearm under this category may be established by evidence of present value and evidence that like firearms are not available except as collector's items, or that the value of like firearms available in ordinary commercial channels is substantially less.

Dealer.

Any person engaged in the business of selling firearms at wholesale or retail; any person engaged in the business of repairing firearms or of making or fitting special barrels, stocks, or trigger mechanisms to firearms; or any person who is a pawnbroker. The term shall include any person who engages in such business or occupation on a part-time basis.

Engaged in the business

a. MANUFACTURER OF FIREARMS.

A person who devotes time, attention, and labor to manufacturing firearms as a regular course of trade or business with the principal objective of livelihood and profit through the sale or distribution of the firearms manufactured;

b. MANUFACTURER OF AMMUNITION.

A person who devotes time, attention, and labor to manufacturing ammunition as a regular course of trade or business with the principal objective of livelihood and profit through the sale or distribution of the ammunition manufactured;

c. DEALER IN FIREARMS OTHER THAN A GUNSMITH OR A PAWNBROKER.

A person who devotes time, attention, and labor to dealing in firearms as a regular course of trade or business with the principal objective of livelihood and profit through the repetitive purchase and resale of firearms, but such a term shall not include a person who makes occasional sales, exchanges, or purchases of firearms for the enhancement of a personal collection or for a hobby, or who sells all or part of his personal collection of firearms;

d. GUNSMITH.

A person who, as a service performed on existing firearms not for sale or distribution, devotes time, attention, and labor to repairing or customizing firearms, making or fitting special barrels, stocks, or trigger mechanisms to firearms, or placing marks of identification on privately made firearms in accordance with this part, as a regular course of trade or business with the principal objective of livelihood and profit, but such a term shall not include a person who occasionally repairs or customizes firearms (including identification), or occasionally makes or fits special barrels, stocks, or trigger mechanisms to firearms. In the case of firearms for purposes of sale or distribution, such term shall include a person who performs repairs (e.g., by replacing worn or broken parts) on complete weapons, or places marks of identification on privately made firearms, but shall not include a person who manufactures firearms (i.e., frames or receivers or complete weapons) by completion, assembly, or applying coatings, or otherwise making them suitable for use, requiring a license as a manufacturer;

e. IMPORTER OF FIREARMS.

A person who devotes time, attention, and labor to importing firearms as a regular course of trade or business with the principal objective of livelihood and profit through the sale or distribution of the firearms imported; and,

f. IMPORTER OF AMMUNITION.

A person who devotes time, attention, and labor to importing ammunition as a regular course of trade or business with the principal objective of livelihood and profit through the sale or distribution of the ammunition imported.

Firearm.

Any weapon, including a starter gun, which will or is designed to or may readily be converted to expel a projectile by the action of an explosive; the frame or receiver of any such weapon; any firearm muffler or firearm silencer; or any destructive device; but the term shall not include an antique firearm. In the case of a licensed collector, the term shall mean only curios and relics. The term shall include a weapon parts kit that is designed to or may readily be completed, assembled, restored, or otherwise converted to expel a projectile by the action of an explosive. The term shall not include a weapon, including a weapon parts kit, in which the frame or receiver of such weapon is destroyed as described in the definition "frame or receiver."

Manufacturer.

Any person engaged in the business of manufacturing firearms or ammunition. The term shall include any person who engages in such business on a part-time basis.

§ 478.102 Sales or deliveries of firearms on and after November 30, 1998.

a. Background check.

Except as provided in paragraph (d) of this section, a licensed importer, licensed manufacturer, or licensed dealer (the licensee) shall not sell, deliver, or transfer a firearm to any other person who is not licensed under this part unless the licensee meets the following requirements:

1. Before the completion of the transfer, the licensee has contacted NICS;

2.

   i. NICS informs the licensee that it has no information that receipt of the firearm by the transferee would be in violation of Federal or State law and provides the licensee with a unique identification number; or

   ii. Three business days (meaning days on which State offices are open) have elapsed from the date the licensee contacted NICS and NICS has not notified the licensee that receipt of the firearm by the transferee would be in violation of law; and

3. The licensee verifies the identity of the transferee by examining the identification document presented in accordance with the provisions of § 478.124(c).

EXAMPLE FOR PARAGRAPH (A).

A licensee contacts NICS on Thursday, and gets a "delayed" response. The licensee does not get a further response from NICS. If State offices are not open on Saturday and Sunday, 3 business days would have elapsed on the following Tuesday. The licensee may transfer the firearm on the next day, Wednesday.

b. Transaction number.

In any transaction for which a licensee receives a transaction number from NICS (which shall include either a NICS transaction number or, in States where the State is recognized as a point of contact for NICS checks, a State transaction number), such number shall be recorded on a firearms transaction record, Form 4473, which shall be retained in the records of the licensee in accordance with the provisions of § 478.129. This applies regardless of whether the transaction is approved or denied by NICS, and regardless of whether the firearm is actually transferred.

c. Time limitation on NICS checks.

A NICS check conducted in accordance with paragraph (a) of this section may be relied upon by the licensee only for use in a single transaction, and for a period not to exceed 30 calendar days from the date that NICS was initially contacted. If the transaction is not completed within the 30-day period, the licensee shall initiate a new NICS check prior to completion of the transfer.

EXAMPLE 1 FOR PARAGRAPH (C).

A purchaser completes the Form 4473 on December 15, 1998, and a NICS check is initiated by the licensee on that date. The licensee is informed by NICS that the information available to the system does not indicate that receipt of the firearm by the transferee would be in violation of law, and a unique identification number is provided. However, the State imposes a 7-day waiting period on all firearms transactions, and the purchaser does not return to pick up the firearm until January 22, 1999. The licensee must conduct another NICS check before transferring the firearm to the purchaser.

EXAMPLE 2 FOR PARAGRAPH (C).

A purchaser completes the Form 4473 on January 25, 1999, and arranges for the purchase of a single firearm. A NICS check is initiated by the licensee on that date. The licensee is informed by NICS that the information available to the system does not indicate that receipt of the firearm by the transferee would be in violation of law, and a unique identification number is provided. The State imposes a 7-day waiting period on all firearms transactions, and the purchaser returns to pick up the firearm on February 15, 1999. Before the licensee executes the Form 4473, and the firearm is transferred, the purchaser decides to purchase an additional firearm. The transfer of these two firearms is considered a single transaction; accordingly, the licensee may add the second firearm to the Form 4473, and transfer that firearm without conducting another NICS check.

EXAMPLE 3 FOR PARAGRAPH (C).

A purchaser completes a Form 4473 on February 15, 1999. The licensee receives a unique identification number from NICS on that date, the Form 4473 is executed by the licensee, and the firearm is transferred. On February 20, 1999, the purchaser returns to the licensee's premises and wishes to purchase a second firearm. The purchase of the second firearm is a separate transaction; thus, a new NICS check must be initiated by the licensee.

d. Exceptions to NICS check.

The provisions of paragraph (a) of this section shall not apply if—

1. The transferee has presented to the licensee a valid permit or license that—

    i. Allows the transferee to possess, acquire, or carry a firearm;

    ii. Was issued not more than 5 years earlier by the State in which the transfer is to take place; and

    iii. The law of the State provides that such a permit or license is to be issued only after an authorized government official has verified that the information available to such official does not indicate that possession of a firearm by the transferee would be in violation of Federal, State, or local law: Provided, That on and after November 30, 1998, the information available to such official includes the NICS;

2. The firearm is subject to the provisions of the National Firearms Act and has been approved for transfer under 27 CFR part 479; or

3. On application of the licensee, in accordance with the provisions of § 478.150, the Director has certified that compliance with paragraph (a)(1) of this section is impracticable.

e. The document referred to in paragraph (d)(1) of this section (or a copy thereof) shall be retained or the required information from the document shall be recorded on the firearms transaction record in accordance with the provisions of § 478.131.

§ 478.104 Secure gun storage or safety device.

a. Any person who applies to be a licensed firearms dealer must certify on ATF Form 7 (5310.12), Application for Federal Firearms License, that compatible secure gun storage or safety devices will be available at any place where firearms are sold under the license to nonlicensed individuals (subject to the exception that in any case in which a secure gun storage or safety device is temporarily unavailable because of theft, casualty, loss, consumer sales, backorders from a manufacturer, or any other similar reason beyond the control of the licensee, the dealer shall not be considered in violation of the requirement to make available such a device).

b. Any person who applies to be a licensed firearms importer or a licensed manufacturer and will be engaged in business on the licensed premises as a dealer in the same type of firearms authorized by the license to be imported or manufactured must make the certification required under paragraph (a) of this section.

c. Each licensee described in this section must have compatible secure gun storage or safety devices available at any place in which firearms are sold under the license to persons who are not licensees. However, such licensee shall not be considered to be in violation of this requirement if a secure gun storage or safety device is temporarily unavailable because of theft, casualty loss, consumer sales, backorders from a manufacturer, or any other similar reason beyond the control of the licensee.

§ 478.121 General.

a. The records pertaining to firearms transactions prescribed by this part shall be retained on the licensed premises in the manner prescribed by this subpart and for the length of time prescribed by § 478.129. The records pertaining to ammunition prescribed by this part shall be retained on the licensed premises in the manner prescribed by § 478.125.

b. ATF officers may, for the purposes and under the conditions prescribed in § 478.23, enter the premises of any licensed importer, licensed manufacturer, licensed dealer, or licensed collector for the purpose of examining or inspecting any record or document required by or obtained under this part. Section 923(g) of the Act requires licensed importers, licensed manufacturers, licensed dealers, and licensed collectors to make such records available for such examination or inspection during business hours or, in the case of licensed collectors, hours of operation, as provided in § 478.23.

c. Each licensed importer, licensed manufacturer, licensed dealer, and licensed collector shall maintain such records of importation, production, shipment, receipt, sale, or other disposition, whether temporary or permanent, of firearms and such records of the disposition of ammunition as the regulations contained in this part prescribe. Section 922(m) of the Act makes it unlawful for any licensed importer, licensed manufacturer, licensed dealer, or licensed collector knowingly to make any false entry in, to fail to make appropriate entry in, or to fail to properly maintain any such record.

d. For recordkeeping requirements for sales by licensees at gun shows see § 478.100(c).

§ 478.123 Records maintained by manufacturers.

a. Except for adjustment or repair of a firearm that is returned to the person from whom it was received on the same day, each licensed manufacturer shall record the name of the manufacturer and importer (if any), type, model, caliber or gauge, and serial number (including any associated license number either as a prefix, or if remanufactured or imported, separated by a semicolon) of each firearm manufactured or otherwise acquired (including a frame or receiver to be disposed of separately), the date of such manufacture or other acquisition, and if otherwise acquired, the name and address or the name and license number of the person from whom it was received. Privately made firearms shall be recorded in accordance with § 478.125(i). The information required by this paragraph shall, in the case of a firearm other than a firearm defined in 26 U.S.C. 5845, be recorded not later than the seventh day following the date of such manufacture or other acquisition. In the case of a firearm defined in 26 U.S.C. 5845, such information shall be recorded by close of the next business day following the date of such manufacture or other acquisition, except that, when a commercial record is held by the licensed manufacturer separately from other commercial documents and readily available for inspection, containing all acquisition information required for the record, the period for making the required entry into the record may be delayed not to exceed the seventh day following the date of receipt. The information required by this paragraph shall be recorded in a format containing the applicable columns prescribed by § 478.122.

b. A record of each firearm disposed of by a manufacturer and a separate record of armor piercing ammunition dispositions to governmental entities, for exportation, or for testing or experimentation authorized under the provisions of § 478.149 shall be maintained by the licensed manufacturer on the licensed premises. The record shall show the date of such sale or other disposition, and the name and license number of the licensee to whom the firearms were transferred, or if disposed of to a nonlicensee, the name and address of the person, or the transaction number of the Firearms Transaction Record, Form 4473, if the licensee transferring the firearm sequentially numbers the Forms 4473 and files them numerically. In the event the licensee records a duplicate entry with the same firearm and acquisition information, whether to close out an old record book or for any other reason, the licensee shall record a reference to the date and location of the subsequent entry (e.g., date of new entry, book name/number, page number, and line number) as the disposition. The information required by this paragraph shall be entered in the proper record book not later than the seventh day following the date of the transaction. Such information shall be recorded in a format containing the applicable columns prescribed by § 478.122, except that for armor piercing ammunition, the information and format shall also include the quantity of projectiles.

c. The Director may authorize alternate records to be maintained by a licensed manufacturer to record the acquisition or disposition of firearms and armor piercing ammunition when it is shown by the licensed manufacturer that such alternate records will accurately and readily disclose the information required by this section. A licensed manufacturer who proposes to use alternate records shall submit a letter application to the Director and shall describe the proposed alternate record and the need therefor. Such alternate records shall not be employed by the licensed manufacturer until approval in such regard is received from the Director.

§ 478.124 Firearms transaction record.

a. A licensed importer, licensed manufacturer, or licensed dealer shall not sell or otherwise dispose, temporarily or permanently, of any firearm to any person, other than another licensee, unless the licensee records the transaction on a firearms transaction record, Form 4473: Provided, That a firearms transaction record, Form 4473, shall not be required to record the disposition made of a firearm delivered to a licensee for the sole purpose of repair or customizing when such firearm or a replacement firearm is returned to the person from whom received.

b. A licensed manufacturer, licensed importer, or licensed dealer shall retain in alphabetical (by name of purchaser), chronological (by date of disposition), or numerical (by transaction number) order, and as a part of the required records, each Form 4473 obtained in the course of transferring custody of the firearms.

c.

1. Prior to making an over-the-counter transfer of a firearm to a nonlicensee who is a resident of the State in which the licensee's business premises is located, the licensed importer, licensed manufacturer, or licensed dealer so transferring the firearm shall obtain a Form 4473 from the transferee showing the transferee's name, sex, residence address (including county or similar political subdivision), date and place of birth; height, weight and race of the transferee; the transferee's country of citizenship; the transferee's INS-issued alien number or admission number; the transferee's State of residence; and certification by the transferee that the transferee is not prohibited by the Act from transporting or shipping a firearm in interstate or foreign commerce or receiving a firearm which has been shipped or transported in interstate or foreign commerce or possessing a firearm in or affecting commerce.

2. In order to facilitate the transfer of a firearm and enable NICS to verify the identity of the person acquiring the firearm, ATF Form 4473 also requests certain optional information. This information includes the transferee's social security number. Such information may help avoid the possibility of the transferee being misidentified as a felon or other prohibited person.

3. After the transferee has executed the Form 4473, the licensee:

i. Shall verify the identity of the transferee by examining the identification document (as defined in § 478.11) presented, and shall note on the Form 4473 the type of identification used;

ii. [Reserved]

iii. Must, in the case of a transferee who is an alien admitted to the United States under a nonimmigrant visa who states that he or she falls within an exception to, or has a waiver from, the prohibition in section 922(g)(5)(B) of the Act, have the transferee present applicable documentation establishing the exception or waiver, note on the Form 4473 the type of documentation provided, and attach a copy of the documentation to the Form 4473; and

iv. Shall comply with the requirements of § 478.102 and record on the form the date on which the licensee contacted the NICS, as well as any response provided by the system, including any identification number provided by the system.

4. The licensee shall identify the firearm to be transferred by listing on the Form 4473 the name of the manufacturer, the name of the importer (if any), the type, model, caliber or gauge, and the serial number (including any associated license number either as a prefix, or if remanufactured or imported, separated by a semicolon) of the firearm. Where no manufacturer name has been identified on a privately made firearm, the words "privately made firearm" (or abbreviation "PMF") shall be recorded as the name of the manufacturer.

5. The licensee shall sign and date the form if the licensee does not know or have reasonable cause to believe that the transferee is disqualified by law from receiving the firearm and transfer the firearm described on the Form 4473.

d. Prior to making an over-the-counter transfer of a shotgun or rifle under the provisions contained in § 478.96(c) to a nonlicensee who is not a resident of the State in which the licensee's business premises is located, the licensee so transferring the shotgun or rifle, and such transferee, shall comply with the requirements of paragraph (c) of this section.

e. Prior to making a transfer of a firearm to any nonlicensee who is not a resident of the State in which the licensee's business premises is located, and such nonlicensee is acquiring the firearm by loan or rental from the licensee for temporary use for lawful sporting purposes, the licensed importer, licensed manufacturer, or licensed dealer so furnishing the firearm, and such transferee, shall comply with the provisions of paragraph (c) of this section.

f. Form 4473 shall be submitted, in duplicate, to a licensed importer, licensed manufacturer, or licensed dealer by a transferee who is purchasing or otherwise acquiring a firearm by other than an over-the-counter transaction, who is not subject to the provisions of § 478.102(a), and who is a resident of the State in which the licensee's business premises are located. The Form 4473 shall show the name, address, date and place of birth, height, weight, and race of the transferee; and the title, name, and address of the principal law enforcement officer of the locality to which the firearm will be delivered. The transferee also must date and execute the sworn statement contained on the form showing, in case the firearm to be transferred is a firearm other than a shotgun or rifle, the transferee is 21 years or more of age; in case the firearm to be transferred is a shotgun or rifle, the transferee is 18 years or more of age; whether the transferee is a citizen of the United States; the transferee's State of residence; the transferee is not prohibited by the provisions of the Act from shipping or transporting a firearm in interstate or foreign commerce or receiving a firearm which has been shipped or transported in interstate or foreign commerce or possessing a firearm in or affecting commerce; and the transferee's receipt of the firearm would not be in violation of any statute of the State or published ordinance applicable to the locality in which the transferee resides. The licensee shall identify the firearm to be transferred by listing in the Forms 4473 the name of the manufacturer, the name of the importer (if any), the type, model, caliber or gauge, and the serial number of the firearm to be transferred. Where no manufacturer name has been identified on a privately made firearm, the words "privately made firearm" (or abbreviation "PMF") shall be recorded as the name of the manufacturer. Postal Service regulations. The original Form 4473, and evidence of receipt or rejection of delivery of the copy of the Form 4473 sent to the principal law enforcement officer, shall be retained by the licensee as a part of the records required to be kept under this subpart.

g. A licensee who sells or otherwise disposes of a firearm to a nonlicensee who is other than an individual, shall obtain from the transferee the information required by this section from an individual authorized to act on behalf of the transferee. In addition, the licensee shall obtain from the individual acting on behalf of the transferee a written statement, executed under the penalties of perjury, that the firearm is being acquired for the use of and will be the property of the transferee, and showing the name and address of that transferee.

h. The requirements of this section shall be in addition to any other recordkeeping requirement contained in this part.

i. A licensee may obtain, upon request, an emergency supply of Forms 4473 from any Director of Industry Operations. For normal usage, a licensee should request a year's supply from the ATF Distribution Center (See § 478.21).

§ 478.125 Record of receipt and disposition.

a. Armor piercing ammunition sales by licensed collectors to nonlicensees.

The sale or other disposition of armor piercing ammunition by licensed collectors shall be recorded in a bound record at the time a transaction is made. The bound record shall be maintained in chronological order by date of sale or disposition of the armor piercing ammunition, and shall be retained on the licensed premises of the licensee for a period not less than two years following the date of the recorded sale or disposition of the armor piercing ammunition. The bound record entry shall show:

1. The date of the transaction;
2. The name of the manufacturer;
3. The caliber or gauge;
4. The quantity of projectiles;
5. The name, address, and date of birth of the nonlicensee; and
6. The method used to establish the identity of the armor piercing ammunition purchaser.

However, when a commercial record is made at the time a transaction is made, a licensee may delay making an entry into the bound record if the provisions of paragraph (d) of this section are complied with.

b. Armor piercing ammunition sales by licensed collectors to licensees.

Sales or other dispositions of armor piercing ammunition from a licensed collector to another licensee shall be recorded and maintained in the manner prescribed in § 478.122(b) for importers: Provided, That the license number of the transferee may be recorded in lieu of the transferee's address.

c. Armor piercing ammunition sales by licensed dealers to governmental entities.

A record of armor piercing ammunition disposed of by a licensed dealer to a governmental entity pursuant to § 478.99(e) shall be maintained by the licensed dealer on the licensed premises and shall show the name of the manufacturer, the caliber or gauge, the quantity, the name and address of the entity to which the armor piercing ammunition was transferred, and the date of the transaction. Such information shall be recorded under the format prescribed by § 478.122(b). Each licensed dealer disposing of armor piercing ammunition pursuant to § 478.99(e) shall also maintain a record showing the date of acquisition of such ammunition which shall be filed in an orderly manner separate from other commercial records maintained and be readily available for inspection. The records required by this paragraph shall be retained on the licensed premises of the licensee for a period not less than two years following the date of the recorded sale or disposition of the armor piercing ammunition.

d. Commercial records of armor piercing ammunition transactions.

When a commercial record is made at the time of sale or other disposition of armor piercing ammunition, and such record contains all information required by the bound record prescribed by paragraph (a) of this section, the licensed collector transferring the armor piercing ammunition may, for a period not exceeding 7 days following the date of such transfer, delay making the required entry into such bound record: Provided, That the commercial record pertaining to the transfer is:

1. Maintained by the licensed collector separate from other commercial documents maintained by such licensee, and
2. Is readily available for inspection on the licensed premises until such time as the required entry into the bound record is made.

e. Firearms receipt and disposition by dealers.

Except for adjustment or repair of a firearm that is returned to the person from whom it was received on the same day, each licensed dealer shall enter into a record each receipt and disposition of firearms. In addition, before commencing or continuing a firearms business, each licensed dealer shall inventory the firearms possessed for such business and shall record the same in the record required by this paragraph. The record required by this paragraph shall be maintained in bound form in the format prescribed below. The purchase or other acquisition of a firearm shall, except as provided in paragraphs (g) and (i) of this section, be recorded not later than the close of the next business day following the date of such purchase or acquisition. The record shall show the date of receipt, the name and address or the name and license number of the person from whom received, the name of the manufacturer and importer (if any), the model, serial number (including any associated license number either as a prefix, or if remanufactured or imported, separated by a semicolon), type, and the caliber or gauge of the firearm. In the event the licensee records a duplicate entry with the same firearm and acquisition information, whether to close out an old record book or for any other reason, the licensee shall record a reference to the date and location of the subsequent entry (e.g., date of new entry, book name/number, page number, and line number) as the disposition. The sale or other disposition of a firearm shall be recorded by the licensed dealer not later than seven days following the date of such transaction. When such disposition is made to a nonlicensee, the firearms transaction record, Form 4473, obtained by the licensed dealer shall be retained, until the transaction is recorded, separate from the licensee's Form 4473 file and be readily available for inspection. When such disposition is made to a licensee, the commercial record of the transaction shall be retained, until the transaction is recorded, separate from other commercial documents maintained by the licensed dealer, and be readily available for inspection. The record shall show the date of the sale or other disposition of each firearm, the name and address of the person to whom the firearm is transferred, or the name and license number of the person to whom transferred if such person is a licensee, or the firearms transaction record, Form 4473, transaction number if the licensed dealer transferring the firearm sequentially numbers the Forms 4473 and files them numerically.

f. Firearms receipt and disposition by licensed collectors.

1. Each licensed collector shall enter into a record each receipt and disposition of firearms curios or relics. The record required by this paragraph shall be maintained in bound form under the format prescribed below. The purchase or other acquisition of a curio or relic shall, except as provided in paragraphs (g) and (i) of this section, be recorded not later than the close of the next business day following the date of such purchase or other acquisition. The record shall show the date of receipt, the name and address or the name and license number of the person from whom received, the name of the manufacturer and importer (if any), the model, serial number (including any associated license number either as a prefix, or if remanufactured or imported, separated by a semicolon), type, and the caliber or gauge of the firearm curio or relic. In the event the licensee records a duplicate entry with the same firearm and acquisition information, whether to close out an old record book or for any other reason, the licensee shall record a reference to the date and location of the subsequent entry (e.g., date of new entry, book name/number, page number, and line number) as the disposition. The sale or other disposition of a curio or relic shall be recorded by the licensed collector not later than seven days following the date of such transaction. When such disposition is made to a licensee, the commercial record of the transaction shall be retained, until the transaction is recorded, separate from other commercial documents maintained by the licensee, and be readily available for inspection. The record shall show the date of the sale or other disposition of each firearm curio or relic, the name and address of the person to whom the firearm curio or relic is transferred, or the name and license number of the person to whom transferred if such person is a licensee, and the date of birth of the transferee if other than a licensee. In addition, the licensee shall cause the transferee, if other than a licensee, to be identified in any manner customarily used in commercial transactions (e.g., a driver's license), and note on the record the method used.

g. Commercial records of firearms received.

When a commercial record is held by a licensed dealer or licensed collector showing the acquisition of a firearm or firearm curio or relic, and such record contains all acquisition information required by the bound record prescribed by paragraphs (e) and (f) of this section, the licensed dealer or licensed collector acquiring such firearm or curio or relic, may, for a period not exceeding 7 days following the date of such acquisition, delay making the required entry into such bound record: Provided, That the commercial record is, until such time as the required entry into the bound record is made, (1) maintained by the licensed dealer or licensed collector separate from other commercial documents maintained by such licensee, and (2) readily available for inspection on the licensed premises: Provided further, That when disposition is made of a firearm or firearm curio or relic not entered in the bound record under the provisions of this paragraph, the licensed dealer or licensed collector making such disposition shall enter all required acquisition information regarding the firearm or firearm curio or relic in the bound record at the time such transfer or disposition is made.

h. Alternate records.

Notwithstanding the provisions of paragraphs (a), (e), and (f) of this section, the Director of Industry Operations may authorize alternate records to be maintained by a licensed dealer or licensed collector to record the acquisition and disposition of firearms or curios or relics and the disposition of armor piercing ammunition when it is shown by the licensed dealer or the licensed collector that such alternate records will accurately and readily disclose the required information. A licensed dealer or licensed collector who proposes to use alternate records shall submit a letter application, in duplicate, to the Director of Industry Operations and shall describe the proposed alternate records and the need therefor. Such alternate records shall not be employed by the licensed dealer or licensed collector until approval in such regard is received from the Director of Industry Operations.

i. Privately made firearms.

Except for adjustment or repair of a firearm that is returned to the person from whom it was received on the same day, licensees must record each receipt or other acquisition (including from a personal collection) and disposition (including to a personal collection) of a privately made firearm as required by this part. For purposes of this paragraph, the terms "receipt" and "acquisition" shall include same-day or on-the-spot placement of identifying markings unless another licensee is placing the markings for, and under the direct supervision of, the licensee who recorded the acquisition. In that case, the licensee placing the markings need not record an acquisition from the supervising licensee or disposition upon return. The serial number need not be immediately recorded if the firearm is being identified by the licensee, or under the licensee's direct supervision with the licensee's serial number, in accordance with § 478.92(a)(2). Once the privately made firearm is so identified, the licensee shall update the record of acquisition entry with the serial number, including the license number prefix, and shall record its disposition in accordance with this section. In this part and part 447, where no manufacturer name has been identified on a privately made firearm (if privately made in the United States), the words "privately made firearm" (or abbreviation "PMF") shall be recorded as the name of the manufacturer.

§ 478.126 Furnishing transaction information.

a. Each licensee shall, when required by letter issued by the Director of Industry Operations, and until notified to the contrary in writing by such officer, submit on Form 5300.5, Report of Firearms Transactions, for the periods and at the times specified in the letter issued by the Director of Industry Operations, all record information required by this subpart, or such lesser record information as the Director of Industry Operations in his letter may specify.

b. The Director of Industry Operations may authorize the information to be submitted in a manner other than that prescribed in paragraph (a) of this section when it is shown by a licensee that an alternate method of reporting is reasonably necessary and will not unduly hinder the effective administration of this part. A licensee who proposes to use an alternate method of reporting shall submit a letter application, in duplicate, to the Director of Industry Operations and shall describe the proposed alternate method of reporting and the need therefor. An alternate method of reporting shall not be employed by the licensee until approval in such regard is received from the Director of Industry Operations.

§ 478.126a Reporting multiple sales or other disposition of pistols and revolvers.

Each licensee shall prepare a report of multiple sales or other disposition whenever the licensee sells or otherwise disposes of, at one time or during any five consecutive business days, two or more pistols, or revolvers, or any combination of pistols and revolvers totaling two or more, to an unlicensed person: Provided, That a report need not be made where pistols or revolvers, or any combination thereof, are returned to the same person from whom they were received. The report shall be prepared on Form 3310.4, Report of Multiple Sale or Other Disposition of Pistols and Revolvers. Not later than the close of business on the day that the multiple sale or other disposition occurs, the licensee shall forward two copies of Form 3310.4 to the ATF office specified thereon and one copy to the State police or to the local law enforcement agency in which the sale or other disposition took place. Where the State or local law enforcement officials have notified the licensee that a particular official has been designated to receive Forms 3310.4, the licensee shall forward such forms to that designated official. The licensee shall retain one copy of Form 3310.4 and attach it to the firearms transaction record, Form 4473, executed upon delivery of the pistols or revolvers.

EXAMPLE. 1.

A licensee sells a pistol and revolver in a single transaction to an unlicensed person. This is a multiple sale and must be reported not later than the close of business on the date of the transaction.

EXAMPLE. 2.

A licensee sells a pistol on Monday and sells a revolver on the following Friday to the same unlicensed person. This is a multiple sale and must be reported not later than the close of business on Friday. If the licensee sells the same unlicensed person another pistol or revolver on the following Monday, this would constitute an additional multiple sale and must also be reported.

EXAMPLE 3.

A licensee maintaining business hours on Monday through Saturday sells a revolver to an unlicensed person on Monday and sells another revolver to the same person on the following Saturday. This does not constitute a multiple sale and need not be reported since the sales did not occur during five consecutive business days.

§ 478.129 Record retention.

a. Records prior to Act.

Licensed importers and licensed manufacturers may dispose of records of sale or other disposition of firearms prior to December 16, 1968. Licensed dealers and licensed collectors may dispose of all records of firearms transactions that occurred prior to December 16, 1968.

b. Firearms Transaction Record.

Licensees shall retain each Form 4473 until business or licensed activity is discontinued, either on paper, or in an electronic alternate method approved by the Director, at the business premises readily accessible for inspection under this part. Paper forms over 20 years of age may be stored at a separate warehouse, which shall be considered part of the business premises for this purpose and subject to inspection under this part. Forms 4473 shall be retained in the licensee's records as provided in § 478.124(b), provided that Forms 4473 with respect to which a sale, delivery, or transfer did not take place shall be separately retained in alphabetical (by name of transferee) or chronological (by date of transferee's certification) order.

c. Statement of intent to obtain a handgun, reports of multiple sales or other disposition of pistols and revolvers, and reports of theft or loss of firearms.

Licensees shall retain each Form 5300.35 (Statement of Intent to Obtain a Handgun(s)) for a period of not less than 5 years after notice of the intent to obtain the handgun was forwarded to the chief law enforcement officer, as defined in § 478.150(c). Licensees shall retain each copy of Form 3310.4 (Report of Multiple Sale or Other Disposition of Pistols and Revolvers) for a period of not less than 5 years after the date of sale or other disposition. Licensees shall retain each copy of Form 3310.11 (Federal Firearms Licensee Theft/Loss Report) for a period of not less than 5 years after the date the theft or loss was reported to ATF.

d. Records of importation and manufacture.

Licensees shall maintain records of the importation, manufacture, or other acquisition of firearms, including ATF Forms 6 and 6A as required by subpart G of this part, until business or licensed activity is discontinued. Licensed importers' records and licensed manufacturers' records of the sale or other disposition of firearms after December 15, 1968, shall be retained until business is discontinued, either on paper or in an electronic alternate method approved by the Director, at the business premises readily accessible for inspection under this part. Paper records that do not contain any open disposition entries and with no dispositions recorded within 20 years may be stored at a separate warehouse, which shall be considered part of the business premises for this purpose and subject to inspection under this part.

e. Records of dealers and collectors.

The records prepared by licensed dealers and licensed collectors of the sale or other disposition of firearms and the corresponding record of receipt of such firearms shall be retained until business or licensed activity is discontinued, either on paper, or in an electronic alternate method approved by the Director, at the business or collection premises readily accessible for inspection under this part. Paper records that do not contain any open disposition entries and with no dispositions recorded within 20 years may be stored at a separate warehouse, which shall be considered part of the business or collection premises for this purpose and subject to inspection under this part.

f. Retention of records of transactions in semiautomatic assault weapons.

The documentation required by §§ 478.40(c) and 478.132 shall be retained in the licensee's permanent records for a period of not less than 5 years after the date of sale or other disposition.

§ 478.131 Firearms transactions not subject to a NICS check.

a.

1. A licensed importer, licensed manufacturer, or licensed dealer whose sale, delivery, or transfer of a firearm is made pursuant to the alternative provisions of § 478.102(d) and is not subject to the NICS check prescribed by § 478.102(a) shall maintain the records required by paragraph (a) of this section.

2. If the transfer is pursuant to a permit or license in accordance with § 478.102(d)(1), the licensee shall either retain a copy of the purchaser's permit or license and attach it to the firearms transaction record, Form 4473, or record on the firearms transaction record, Form 4473, any identifying number, the date of issuance, and the expiration date (if provided) from the permit or license.

3. If the transfer is pursuant to a certification by ATF in accordance with §§ 478.102(d)(3) and 478.150, the licensee shall maintain the certification as part of the records required to be kept under this subpart and for the period prescribed for the retention of Form 5300.35 in § 478.129(c).

b. The requirements of this section shall be in addition to any other recordkeeping requirements contained in this part.

Description of Firearm					
No.	Manufacturer, Importer (if any), or "Privately Made Firearm" (PMF)	Model	Serial Number	Type	Caliber or Gauge
1					
2					
3					
4					
5					
6					
7					
8					
9					
10					
11					
12					
13					
14					
15					
16					
17					
18					
19					
20					

Receipt		Disposition			
Acquisition Date	Name/Address of Non-Licensee; or Licensee Name/No.	Disposition Date	Recipient Name	Address of Non-Licensee or License No., or 4473 Trans. No. if filed numerically	Ref #

Description of Firearm					
No.	Manufacturer, Importer (if any), or "Privately Made Firearm" (PMF)	Model	Serial Number	Type	Caliber or Gauge
21					
22					
23					
24					
25					
26					
27					
28					
29					
30					
31					
32					
33					
34					
35					
36					
37					
38					
39					
40					

Receipt		Disposition			
Acquisition Date	Name/Address of Non-Licensee; or Licensee Name/No.	Disposition Date	Recipient Name	Address of Non-Licensee or License No., or 4473 Trans. No. if filed numerically	Ref #

Description of Firearm					
No.	Manufacturer, Importer (if any), or "Privately Made Firearm" (PMF)	Model	Serial Number	Type	Caliber or Gauge
41					
42					
43					
44					
45					
46					
47					
48					
49					
50					
51					
52					
53					
54					
55					
56					
57					
58					
59					
60					

Receipt		Disposition			
Acquisition Date	Name/Address of Non-Licensee; or Licensee Name/No.	Disposition Date	Recipient Name	Address of Non-Licensee or License No., or 4473 Trans. No. if filed numerically	Ref #

Description of Firearm					
No.	Manufacturer, Importer (if any), or "Privately Made Firearm" (PMF)	Model	Serial Number	Type	Caliber or Gauge
61					
62					
63					
64					
65					
66					
67					
68					
69					
70					
71					
72					
73					
74					
75					
76					
77					
78					
79					
80					

Receipt		Disposition			
Acquisition Date	Name/Address of Non-Licensee; or Licensee Name/No.	Disposition Date	Recipient Name	Address of Non-Licensee or License No., or 4473 Trans. No. if filed numerically	Ref #

Description of Firearm					
No.	Manufacturer, Importer (if any), or "Privately Made Firearm" (PMF)	Model	Serial Number	Type	Caliber or Gauge
81					
82					
83					
84					
85					
86					
87					
88					
89					
90					
91					
92					
93					
94					
95					
96					
97					
98					
99					
100					

Receipt		Disposition			
Acquisition Date	Name/Address of Non-Licensee; or Licensee Name/No.	Disposition Date	Recipient Name	Address of Non-Licensee or License No., or 4473 Trans. No. if filed numerically	Ref #

Description of Firearm					
No.	Manufacturer, Importer (if any), or "Privately Made Firearm" (PMF)	Model	Serial Number	Type	Caliber or Gauge
101					
102					
103					
104					
105					
106					
107					
108					
109					
110					
111					
112					
113					
114					
115					
116					
117					
118					
119					
120					

Receipt		Disposition			
Acquisition Date	Name/Address of Non-Licensee; or Licensee Name/No.	Disposition Date	Recipient Name	Address of Non-Licensee or License No., or 4473 Trans. No. if filed numerically	Ref #

Description of Firearm					
No.	Manufacturer, Importer (if any), or "Privately Made Firearm" (PMF)	Model	Serial Number	Type	Caliber or Gauge
121					
122					
123					
124					
125					
126					
127					
128					
129					
130					
131					
132					
133					
134					
135					
136					
137					
138					
139					
140					

Receipt		Disposition			
Acquisition Date	Name/Address of Non-Licensee; or Licensee Name/No.	Disposition Date	Recipient Name	Address of Non-Licensee or License No., or 4473 Trans. No. if filed numerically	Ref #

Description of Firearm					
No.	Manufacturer, Importer (if any), or "Privately Made Firearm" (PMF)	Model	Serial Number	Type	Caliber or Gauge
141					
142					
143					
144					
145					
146					
147					
148					
149					
150					
151					
152					
153					
154					
155					
156					
157					
158					
159					
160					

Receipt		Disposition			
Acquisition Date	Name/Address of Non-Licensee; or Licensee Name/No.	Disposition Date	Recipient Name	Address of Non-Licensee or License No., or 4473 Trans. No. if filed numerically	Ref #

Description of Firearm					
No.	Manufacturer, Importer (if any), or "Privately Made Firearm" (PMF)	Model	Serial Number	Type	Caliber or Gauge
161					
162					
163					
164					
165					
166					
167					
168					
169					
170					
171					
172					
173					
174					
175					
176					
177					
178					
179					
180					

Receipt		Disposition			
Acquisition Date	Name/Address of Non-Licensee; or Licensee Name/No.	Disposition Date	Recipient Name	Address of Non-Licensee or License No., or 4473 Trans. No. if filed numerically	Ref #

Description of Firearm					
No.	Manufacturer, Importer (if any), or "Privately Made Firearm" (PMF)	Model	Serial Number	Type	Caliber or Gauge
181					
182					
183					
184					
185					
186					
187					
188					
189					
190					
191					
192					
193					
194					
195					
196					
197					
198					
199					
200					

Receipt		Disposition			
Acquisition Date	Name/Address of Non-Licensee; or Licensee Name/No.	Disposition Date	Recipient Name	Address of Non-Licensee or License No., or 4473 Trans. No. if filed numerically	Ref #

Description of Firearm					
No.	Manufacturer, Importer (if any), or "Privately Made Firearm" (PMF)	Model	Serial Number	Type	Caliber or Gauge
201					
202					
203					
204					
205					
206					
207					
208					
209					
210					
211					
212					
213					
214					
215					
216					
217					
218					
219					
220					

Receipt		Disposition			
Acquisition Date	Name/Address of Non-Licensee; or Licensee Name/No.	Disposition Date	Recipient Name	Address of Non-Licensee or License No., or 4473 Trans. No. if filed numerically	Ref #

Description of Firearm					
No.	Manufacturer, Importer (if any), or "Privately Made Firearm" (PMF)	Model	Serial Number	Type	Caliber or Gauge
221					
222					
223					
224					
225					
226					
227					
228					
229					
230					
231					
232					
233					
234					
235					
236					
237					
238					
239					
240					

Receipt		Disposition			
Acquisition Date	Name/Address of Non-Licensee; or Licensee Name/No.	Disposition Date	Recipient Name	Address of Non-Licensee or License No., or 4473 Trans. No. if filed numerically	Ref #

Description of Firearm					
No.	Manufacturer, Importer (if any), or "Privately Made Firearm" (PMF)	Model	Serial Number	Type	Caliber or Gauge
241					
242					
243					
244					
245					
246					
247					
248					
249					
250					
251					
252					
253					
254					
255					
256					
257					
258					
259					
260					

Receipt		Disposition			
Acquisition Date	Name/Address of Non-Licensee; or Licensee Name/No.	Disposition Date	Recipient Name	Address of Non-Licensee or License No., or 4473 Trans. No. if filed numerically	Ref #

Description of Firearm					
No.	Manufacturer, Importer (if any), or "Privately Made Firearm" (PMF)	Model	Serial Number	Type	Caliber or Gauge
261					
262					
263					
264					
265					
266					
267					
268					
269					
270					
271					
272					
273					
274					
275					
276					
277					
278					
279					
280					

Receipt		Disposition			
Acquisition Date	Name/Address of Non-Licensee; or Licensee Name/No.	Disposition Date	Recipient Name	Address of Non-Licensee or License No., or 4473 Trans. No. if filed numerically	Ref #

Description of Firearm					
No.	Manufacturer, Importer (if any), or "Privately Made Firearm" (PMF)	Model	Serial Number	Type	Caliber or Gauge
281					
282					
283					
284					
285					
286					
287					
288					
289					
290					
291					
292					
293					
294					
295					
296					
297					
298					
299					
300					

Receipt		Disposition			
Acquisition Date	Name/Address of Non-Licensee; or Licensee Name/No.	Disposition Date	Recipient Name	Address of Non-Licensee or License No., or 4473 Trans. No. if filed numerically	Ref #

Description of Firearm					
No.	Manufacturer, Importer (if any), or "Privately Made Firearm" (PMF)	Model	Serial Number	Type	Caliber or Gauge
301					
302					
303					
304					
305					
306					
307					
308					
309					
310					
311					
312					
313					
314					
315					
316					
317					
318					
319					
320					

Receipt		Disposition			
Acquisition Date	Name/Address of Non-Licensee; or Licensee Name/No.	Disposition Date	Recipient Name	Address of Non-Licensee or License No., or 4473 Trans. No. if filed numerically	Ref #

Description of Firearm					
No.	Manufacturer, Importer (if any), or "Privately Made Firearm" (PMF)	Model	Serial Number	Type	Caliber or Gauge
321					
322					
323					
324					
325					
326					
327					
328					
329					
330					
331					
332					
333					
334					
335					
336					
337					
338					
339					
340					

Receipt		Disposition			
Acquisition Date	Name/Address of Non-Licensee; or Licensee Name/No.	Disposition Date	Recipient Name	Address of Non-Licensee or License No., or 4473 Trans. No. if filed numerically	Ref #

Description of Firearm					
No.	Manufacturer, Importer (if any), or "Privately Made Firearm" (PMF)	Model	Serial Number	Type	Caliber or Gauge
341					
342					
343					
344					
345					
346					
347					
348					
349					
350					
351					
352					
353					
354					
355					
356					
357					
358					
359					
360					

Receipt		Disposition			
Acquisition Date	Name/Address of Non-Licensee; or Licensee Name/No.	Disposition Date	Recipient Name	Address of Non-Licensee or License No., or 4473 Trans. No. if filed numerically	Ref #

Description of Firearm					
No.	Manufacturer, Importer (if any), or "Privately Made Firearm" (PMF)	Model	Serial Number	Type	Caliber or Gauge
361					
362					
363					
364					
365					
366					
367					
368					
369					
370					
371					
372					
373					
374					
375					
376					
377					
378					
379					
380					

Receipt		Disposition			
Acquisition Date	Name/Address of Non-Licensee; or Licensee Name/No.	Disposition Date	Recipient Name	Address of Non-Licensee or License No., or 4473 Trans. No. if filed numerically	Ref #

Description of Firearm					
No.	Manufacturer, Importer (if any), or "Privately Made Firearm" (PMF)	Model	Serial Number	Type	Caliber or Gauge
381					
382					
383					
384					
385					
386					
387					
388					
389					
390					
391					
392					
393					
394					
395					
396					
397					
398					
399					
400					

Receipt		Disposition			
Acquisition Date	Name/Address of Non-Licensee; or Licensee Name/No.	Disposition Date	Recipient Name	Address of Non-Licensee or License No., or 4473 Trans. No. if filed numerically	Ref #

Description of Firearm					
No.	Manufacturer, Importer (if any), or "Privately Made Firearm" (PMF)	Model	Serial Number	Type	Caliber or Gauge
401					
402					
403					
404					
405					
406					
407					
408					
409					
410					
411					
412					
413					
414					
415					
416					
417					
418					
419					
420					

Receipt		Disposition			
Acquisition Date	Name/Address of Non-Licensee; or Licensee Name/No.	Disposition Date	Recipient Name	Address of Non-Licensee or License No., or 4473 Trans. No. if filed numerically	Ref #

Description of Firearm					
No.	Manufacturer, Importer (if any), or "Privately Made Firearm" (PMF)	Model	Serial Number	Type	Caliber or Gauge
421					
422					
423					
424					
425					
426					
427					
428					
429					
430					
431					
432					
433					
434					
435					
436					
437					
438					
439					
440					

Receipt		Disposition			
Acquisition Date	Name/Address of Non-Licensee; or Licensee Name/No.	Disposition Date	Recipient Name	Address of Non-Licensee or License No., or 4473 Trans. No. if filed numerically	Ref #

Description of Firearm					
No.	Manufacturer, Importer (if any), or "Privately Made Firearm" (PMF)	Model	Serial Number	Type	Caliber or Gauge
441					
442					
443					
444					
445					
446					
447					
448					
449					
450					
451					
452					
453					
454					
455					
456					
457					
458					
459					
460					

Receipt		Disposition			
Acquisition Date	Name/Address of Non-Licensee; or Licensee Name/No.	Disposition Date	Recipient Name	Address of Non-Licensee or License No., or 4473 Trans. No. if filed numerically	Ref #

Description of Firearm					
No.	Manufacturer, Importer (if any), or "Privately Made Firearm" (PMF)	Model	Serial Number	Type	Caliber or Gauge
461					
462					
463					
464					
465					
466					
467					
468					
469					
470					
471					
472					
473					
474					
475					
476					
477					
478					
479					
480					

Receipt		Disposition			
Acquisition Date	Name/Address of Non-Licensee; or Licensee Name/No.	Disposition Date	Recipient Name	Address of Non-Licensee or License No., or 4473 Trans. No. if filed numerically	Ref #

Description of Firearm					
No.	Manufacturer, Importer (if any), or "Privately Made Firearm" (PMF)	Model	Serial Number	Type	Caliber or Gauge
481					
482					
483					
484					
485					
486					
487					
488					
489					
490					
491					
492					
493					
494					
495					
496					
497					
498					
499					
500					

Receipt		Disposition			
Acquisition Date	Name/Address of Non-Licensee; or Licensee Name/No.	Disposition Date	Recipient Name	Address of Non-Licensee or License No., or 4473 Trans. No. if filed numerically	Ref #

Description of Firearm					
No.	Manufacturer, Importer (if any), or "Privately Made Firearm" (PMF)	Model	Serial Number	Type	Caliber or Gauge
501					
502					
503					
504					
505					
506					
507					
508					
509					
510					
511					
512					
513					
514					
515					
516					
517					
518					
519					
520					

Receipt		Disposition			
Acquisition Date	Name/Address of Non-Licensee; or Licensee Name/No.	Disposition Date	Recipient Name	Address of Non-Licensee or License No., or 4473 Trans. No. if filed numerically	Ref #

Description of Firearm					
No.	Manufacturer, Importer (if any), or "Privately Made Firearm" (PMF)	Model	Serial Number	Type	Caliber or Gauge
521					
522					
523					
524					
525					
526					
527					
528					
529					
530					
531					
532					
533					
534					
535					
536					
537					
538					
539					
540					

Receipt		Disposition			
Acquisition Date	Name/Address of Non-Licensee; or Licensee Name/No.	Disposition Date	Recipient Name	Address of Non-Licensee or License No., or 4473 Trans. No. if filed numerically	Ref #

Description of Firearm					
No.	Manufacturer, Importer (if any), or "Privately Made Firearm" (PMF)	Model	Serial Number	Type	Caliber or Gauge
541					
542					
543					
544					
545					
546					
547					
548					
549					
550					
551					
552					
553					
554					
555					
556					
557					
558					
559					
560					

Receipt		Disposition			
Acquisition Date	Name/Address of Non-Licensee; or Licensee Name/No.	Disposition Date	Recipient Name	Address of Non-Licensee or License No., or 4473 Trans. No. if filed numerically	Ref #

Description of Firearm					
No.	Manufacturer, Importer (if any), or "Privately Made Firearm" (PMF)	Model	Serial Number	Type	Caliber or Gauge
561					
562					
563					
564					
565					
566					
567					
568					
569					
570					
571					
572					
573					
574					
575					
576					
577					
578					
579					
580					

Receipt		Disposition			
Acquisition Date	Name/Address of Non-Licensee; or Licensee Name/No.	Disposition Date	Recipient Name	Address of Non-Licensee or License No., or 4473 Trans. No. if filed numerically	Ref #

Description of Firearm					
No.	Manufacturer, Importer (if any), or "Privately Made Firearm" (PMF)	Model	Serial Number	Type	Caliber or Gauge
581					
582					
583					
584					
585					
586					
587					
588					
589					
590					
591					
592					
593					
594					
595					
596					
597					
598					
599					
600					

Receipt		Disposition			
Acquisition Date	Name/Address of Non-Licensee; or Licensee Name/No.	Disposition Date	Recipient Name	Address of Non-Licensee or License No., or 4473 Trans. No. if filed numerically	Ref #

Description of Firearm					
No.	Manufacturer, Importer (if any), or "Privately Made Firearm" (PMF)	Model	Serial Number	Type	Caliber or Gauge
601					
602					
603					
604					
605					
606					
607					
608					
609					
610					
611					
612					
613					
614					
615					
616					
617					
618					
619					
620					

Receipt		Disposition			
Acquisition Date	Name/Address of Non-Licensee; or Licensee Name/No.	Disposition Date	Recipient Name	Address of Non-Licensee or License No., or 4473 Trans. No. if filed numerically	Ref #

Description of Firearm					
No.	Manufacturer, Importer (if any), or "Privately Made Firearm" (PMF)	Model	Serial Number	Type	Caliber or Gauge
621					
622					
623					
624					
625					
626					
627					
628					
629					
630					
631					
632					
633					
634					
635					
636					
637					
638					
639					
640					

Receipt		Disposition			
Acquisition Date	Name/Address of Non-Licensee; or Licensee Name/No.	Disposition Date	Recipient Name	Address of Non-Licensee or License No., or 4473 Trans. No. if filed numerically	Ref #

Description of Firearm					
No.	Manufacturer, Importer (if any), or "Privately Made Firearm" (PMF)	Model	Serial Number	Type	Caliber or Gauge
641					
642					
643					
644					
645					
646					
647					
648					
649					
650					
651					
652					
653					
654					
655					
656					
657					
658					
659					
660					

Receipt		Disposition			
Acquisition Date	Name/Address of Non-Licensee; or Licensee Name/No.	Disposition Date	Recipient Name	Address of Non-Licensee or License No., or 4473 Trans. No. if filed numerically	Ref #

Description of Firearm					
No.	Manufacturer, Importer (if any), or "Privately Made Firearm" (PMF)	Model	Serial Number	Type	Caliber or Gauge
661					
662					
663					
664					
665					
666					
667					
668					
669					
670					
671					
672					
673					
674					
675					
676					
677					
678					
679					
680					

Receipt		Disposition			
Acquisition Date	Name/Address of Non-Licensee; or Licensee Name/No.	Disposition Date	Recipient Name	Address of Non-Licensee or License No., or 4473 Trans. No. if filed numerically	Ref #

Description of Firearm					
No.	Manufacturer, Importer (if any), or "Privately Made Firearm" (PMF)	Model	Serial Number	Type	Caliber or Gauge
681					
682					
683					
684					
685					
686					
687					
688					
689					
690					
691					
692					
693					
694					
695					
696					
697					
698					
699					
700					

Receipt		Disposition			
Acquisition Date	Name/Address of Non-Licensee; or Licensee Name/No.	Disposition Date	Recipient Name	Address of Non-Licensee or License No., or 4473 Trans. No. if filed numerically	Ref #

Description of Firearm					
No.	Manufacturer, Importer (if any), or "Privately Made Firearm" (PMF)	Model	Serial Number	Type	Caliber or Gauge
701					
702					
703					
704					
705					
706					
707					
708					
709					
710					
711					
712					
713					
714					
715					
716					
717					
718					
719					
720					

Receipt		Disposition			
Acquisition Date	Name/Address of Non-Licensee; or Licensee Name/No.	Disposition Date	Recipient Name	Address of Non-Licensee or License No., or 4473 Trans. No. if filed numerically	Ref #

Description of Firearm					
No.	Manufacturer, Importer (if any), or "Privately Made Firearm" (PMF)	Model	Serial Number	Type	Caliber or Gauge
721					
722					
723					
724					
725					
726					
727					
728					
729					
730					
731					
732					
733					
734					
735					
736					
737					
738					
739					
740					

Receipt		Disposition			
Acquisition Date	Name/Address of Non-Licensee; or Licensee Name/No.	Disposition Date	Recipient Name	Address of Non-Licensee or License No., or 4473 Trans. No. if filed numerically	Ref #

Description of Firearm					
No.	Manufacturer, Importer (if any), or "Privately Made Firearm" (PMF)	Model	Serial Number	Type	Caliber or Gauge
741					
742					
743					
744					
745					
746					
747					
748					
749					
750					
751					
752					
753					
754					
755					
756					
757					
758					
759					
760					

Receipt		Disposition			
Acquisition Date	Name/Address of Non-Licensee; or Licensee Name/No.	Disposition Date	Recipient Name	Address of Non-Licensee or License No., or 4473 Trans. No. if filed numerically	Ref #

Description of Firearm					
No.	Manufacturer, Importer (if any), or "Privately Made Firearm" (PMF)	Model	Serial Number	Type	Caliber or Gauge
761					
762					
763					
764					
765					
766					
767					
768					
769					
770					
771					
772					
773					
774					
775					
776					
777					
778					
779					
780					

Receipt		Disposition			
Acquisition Date	Name/Address of Non-Licensee; or Licensee Name/No.	Disposition Date	Recipient Name	Address of Non-Licensee or License No., or 4473 Trans. No. if filed numerically	Ref #

Description of Firearm					
No.	Manufacturer, Importer (if any), or "Privately Made Firearm" (PMF)	Model	Serial Number	Type	Caliber or Gauge
781					
782					
783					
784					
785					
786					
787					
788					
789					
790					
791					
792					
793					
794					
795					
796					
797					
798					
799					
800					

Receipt		Disposition			
Acquisition Date	Name/Address of Non-Licensee; or Licensee Name/No.	Disposition Date	Recipient Name	Address of Non-Licensee or License No., or 4473 Trans. No. if filed numerically	Ref #

Description of Firearm					
No.	Manufacturer, Importer (if any), or "Privately Made Firearm" (PMF)	Model	Serial Number	Type	Caliber or Gauge
801					
802					
803					
804					
805					
806					
807					
808					
809					
810					
811					
812					
813					
814					
815					
816					
817					
818					
819					
820					

Receipt		Disposition			
Acquisition Date	Name/Address of Non-Licensee; or Licensee Name/No.	Disposition Date	Recipient Name	Address of Non-Licensee or License No., or 4473 Trans. No. if filed numerically	Ref #

Description of Firearm					
No.	Manufacturer, Importer (if any), or "Privately Made Firearm" (PMF)	Model	Serial Number	Type	Caliber or Gauge
821					
822					
823					
824					
825					
826					
827					
828					
829					
830					
831					
832					
833					
834					
835					
836					
837					
838					
839					
840					

Receipt		Disposition			
Acquisition Date	Name/Address of Non-Licensee; or Licensee Name/No.	Disposition Date	Recipient Name	Address of Non-Licensee or License No., or 4473 Trans. No. if filed numerically	Ref #

Description of Firearm					
No.	Manufacturer, Importer (if any), or "Privately Made Firearm" (PMF)	Model	Serial Number	Type	Caliber or Gauge
841					
842					
843					
844					
845					
846					
847					
848					
849					
850					
851					
852					
853					
854					
855					
856					
857					
858					
859					
860					

Receipt		Disposition			
Acquisition Date	Name/Address of Non-Licensee; or Licensee Name/No.	Disposition Date	Recipient Name	Address of Non-Licensee or License No., or 4473 Trans. No. if filed numerically	Ref #

Description of Firearm					
No.	Manufacturer, Importer (if any), or "Privately Made Firearm" (PMF)	Model	Serial Number	Type	Caliber or Gauge
861					
862					
863					
864					
865					
866					
867					
868					
869					
870					
871					
872					
873					
874					
875					
876					
877					
878					
879					
880					

Receipt		Disposition			
Acquisition Date	Name/Address of Non-Licensee; or Licensee Name/No.	Disposition Date	Recipient Name	Address of Non-Licensee or License No., or 4473 Trans. No. if filed numerically	Ref #

Description of Firearm					
No.	Manufacturer, Importer (if any), or "Privately Made Firearm" (PMF)	Model	Serial Number	Type	Caliber or Gauge
881					
882					
883					
884					
885					
886					
887					
888					
889					
890					
891					
892					
893					
894					
895					
896					
897					
898					
899					
900					

Receipt		Disposition			
Acquisition Date	Name/Address of Non-Licensee; or Licensee Name/No.	Disposition Date	Recipient Name	Address of Non-Licensee or License No., or 4473 Trans. No. if filed numerically	Ref #

Description of Firearm					
No.	Manufacturer, Importer (if any), or "Privately Made Firearm" (PMF)	Model	Serial Number	Type	Caliber or Gauge
901					
902					
903					
904					
905					
906					
907					
908					
909					
910					
911					
912					
913					
914					
915					
916					
917					
918					
919					
920					

Receipt		Disposition			
Acquisition Date	Name/Address of Non-Licensee; or Licensee Name/No.	Disposition Date	Recipient Name	Address of Non-Licensee or License No., or 4473 Trans. No. if filed numerically	Ref #

Description of Firearm					
No.	Manufacturer, Importer (if any), or "Privately Made Firearm" (PMF)	Model	Serial Number	Type	Caliber or Gauge
921					
922					
923					
924					
925					
926					
927					
928					
929					
930					
931					
932					
933					
934					
935					
936					
937					
938					
939					
940					

Receipt		Disposition			
Acquisition Date	Name/Address of Non-Licensee; or Licensee Name/No.	Disposition Date	Recipient Name	Address of Non-Licensee or License No., or 4473 Trans. No. if filed numerically	Ref #

Description of Firearm					
No.	Manufacturer, Importer (if any), or "Privately Made Firearm" (PMF)	Model	Serial Number	Type	Caliber or Gauge
941					
942					
943					
944					
945					
946					
947					
948					
949					
950					
951					
952					
953					
954					
955					
956					
957					
958					
959					
960					

Receipt		Disposition			
Acquisition Date	Name/Address of Non-Licensee; or Licensee Name/No.	Disposition Date	Recipient Name	Address of Non-Licensee or License No., or 4473 Trans. No. if filed numerically	Ref #

Description of Firearm					
No.	Manufacturer, Importer (if any), or "Privately Made Firearm" (PMF)	Model	Serial Number	Type	Caliber or Gauge
961					
962					
963					
964					
965					
966					
967					
968					
969					
970					
971					
972					
973					
974					
975					
976					
977					
978					
979					
980					

Receipt		Disposition			
Acquisition Date	Name/Address of Non-Licensee; or Licensee Name/No.	Disposition Date	Recipient Name	Address of Non-Licensee or License No., or 4473 Trans. No. if filed numerically	Ref #

Description of Firearm					
No.	Manufacturer, Importer (if any), or "Privately Made Firearm" (PMF)	Model	Serial Number	Type	Caliber or Gauge
981					
982					
983					
984					
985					
986					
987					
988					
989					
990					
991					
992					
993					
994					
995					
996					
997					
998					
999					
1000					

Receipt		Disposition			
Acquisition Date	Name/Address of Non-Licensee; or Licensee Name/No.	Disposition Date	Recipient Name	Address of Non-Licensee or License No., or 4473 Trans. No. if filed numerically	Ref #

Made in the USA
Monee, IL
09 May 2026

ec3b419b-e311-4649-b58d-27715b351f3bR01